Poem On Education

By

Aham

Qurate
quratebooks.com

POEM ON EDUCATION
Aham

Published in 2025

© Published by

Qurate Books Pvt. Ltd.
Goa 403523, India
www.quratebooks.com
Tel: 1800-210-6527, Email: info@quratebooks.com

ISBN: 978-93-58986-21-1

EDUCATION

Know way to answer
And way is direction

Way

A
At start of way
One sees twelve
And these twelve
Have own individuality
One sees twelve's individuality

Twelve one after another
And at first is TRUTH

1. *All exist are Truth*
   We feel sees touch

2. *Three forms of this existence*
   And show direction or directionless
   Form of content
   Form of content less
   Form as surround force

3. *These three forms*
   With their own form
   And lives for certain time

4. *Form which appear it also disappear*
   Matter with action
   Form making form regenerate
   By disappearing another form

5. *We some are content*

6. *One who is content*
Have eyes
To see peace
To last

7. *Satkar*
A Creator
Mother father
Pedda pedda k
(As) Mother Earth (As) Father Sun
Respect to all

With
A Pram
If you are
Respect to you

A Deva
If you are
Respect to you

A All
Respect to all

At second is OBJECT and ITS PLACE

1. *All objects are somewhere*
   And this somewhere
   Their place

2. *We see stars above*
   And they are
   Only there

3. *We see Sun Moon*
   And they are
   Where they are

4. *All things*
   On (As) Mother Earth Surface
   They are only
   On (As) Mother Earth Surface

5. *Birds fly in air*
And they fly
Only in air

6. *Fish swim in water*
And fish swim
Only in water

7. *Cloud shifts in air*
And cloud shift
Only in air

At third is CONDITION and CREATE

1. *Condition on matter do create*

2. *(As) Father Sun*
   Gives light and warm
   To (As) Mother Earth
   And (As) Mother Earth
   Form forms
   Of growth shift (may not)
   And regenerate

3. *On (As) Father Sun set*
   All are silent
   Birds gather on tree
   And silent

4. *All attract*
   To (As) Father Sun light

5. *Flying insects fly*
To lamp light
In night

6. *These trees*
Grow to upward

7. *We feels*
Good in day

8. *May (As) Mother Earth*
Have attachment
With (As) Father Sun rays
And (As) Father Sun rays
With (As) Mother Earth
Both try to unite

At fourth is HUMAN TOGETHERNESS

1. *Consciousness of To Be of person*
   When wife and husband are together

2. *Wife and husband*
   They are together
   By feelings and of embrace

3. *They lives*
   Permanently in union
   And all lives
   This way
   Which the
   Order of society

4. *Their children*
   And non interest interaction
   By people
   Are other togetherness

5. *Wife and husband*
Living together permanently
By feelings

6. *Beauty innocence and righteousness*
Gives symmetry
Symmetry raise respect
Respect raise attraction
Attraction forms belief
Belief put sacrifice
Then comes feel good
This relation between two
Is Eeayedakhatrraha
And the embrace
Of these two
To unite
Permanently to
In one

7. *All lives in this way*

8. *Wife and husband*
Increase happiness
By their newborn
And all do so

9. *The newborn*
Takes birth
And lives
For a time
With their
Mother Father

10. *The newborn*
Lives with
Mother Father
Grow young
And seek
Its partner

11. *Mother Father*
Live with
Newborn
Newborn
By innocence and beauty
Gives symmetry
Symmetry raise respect
Respect raise attraction
Attraction put sacrifice
Then comes feel good

This relation
Between parent and children
Is Ayeetrraha

12. *Child feels same*

13. *All lives in this way*

14. *A family and other families*
A family lives
Nearby other families

15. *A family lives*
By feelings
Innocence and beauty
Gives symmetry
Symmetry raises Respect
Respect raises attraction
Attraction forms
Mercy or help
This relation
Between families
Is Ayeegya

16. *Families live*
By non interest relation

17. *Families live*
By call
Same age
The sister
And the brother

18. *Families live*
By call
Elder
The elder

19. *Families live*
By call
Young
The young

20. *Public places*
Clearly mark
For family only
Women only
And men only

21. *Working places*
Clearly segregate
By time
Women in morning
And men in evening

22. *You will have all respects*
And you live where he live

23. *Marriage*
A vow of two
Living together permanently
To whole life
in presence
Of clean fire
Families and other known
To occur
Feelings and embrace
And permanent dip
To feel good

At fifth is HUMAN CONSUMPTION

1. *We live*
   By food
   Food come
   By many things
   These all
   In consumption

2. *We live*
   By cloth
   Cloth come
   By many things
   These all
   In consumption

3. *We live*
   By house
   House is

By many things
These all
In consumption

4. *We live*
By knowledge
Knowledge come
By many things
These all
In consumption

5. *We live*
By medicine and recovery
Medicine and recovery
Are by many things
These all
In consumption

6. *We live*
By other things
Other things
Are by many things
These all
In consumption

7. *We are by*
Vital consumption

At sixth is HUMAN WORKING POWER

1. *We ends energy*
   To do work
   For own

2. *Certain amount*
   Of energy ends
   For complete
   Certain type
   Of work

3. *Young can*
   Do physical work
   Efficiently
   Than older

4. *Work should*
   Given on
   Age base
   In academics

With equal wage or value
To all

5. *The manner*
To complete work
Habit of
Slow continuous
And bodily active

6. *Habit of working*
Should present
In one

At seventh is HUMAN EDUCATION

1. *Know way to answer*
   And way is direction

2. *In the way*

3. *One knowing*
   Observation
   By silence
   And control
   Unlike feelings

4. *One dealing*
   Interpretation
   And selecting
   Right interpretation
   For need

5. *One follow*
   Griefless path
   Fulfil need
   With dedication

6. *Needs*
   Are twelve

7. *Direction of life*
   Reflect in Truth
   Where form
   Is content

8. *We practice moral*
   For search peace
   To last

9. *May all*
   Struggle for peace
   Whether they
   Recognise or not
   Direction of life

10. *May peace is Final stop*

At eighth is HUMAN POPULATION

1. *Population course is*
   An active phenomenon

2. *Population course*
   At stability
   When two born
   From their parent
   At the age
   Of grand or elders
   Are full

3. *Women respect*
   May help in
   Population course stability

4. *Population course and*
   Population course stability
   Depend on us

5. *Three population courses*

6. *When population course*
In extreme decline
May extinct
Human species
The space dangers
(As) Mother earth sadness
Bodily diseases or disorders
May less in research

7. *When population course*
Population at number
Research is happening
Save from
Space dangers
(As) Mother earth sadness
And diseases or disorders

8. *When population course*
Population at high number
May distract to see
Space dangers

(As) Mother earth sadness
Bodily diseases and disorders
In maintained calm
And easy life
To ponder Truth -
Form of content
And practice morals

At ninth is HUMAN DEFENCE

1. *Four things come here*

2. *Look regular to space dangers*

3. *Look regular to (As) Mother earth sadness*
   Home (As) Mother Earth
   To live
   When profuse in green
   Dark blue sky
   Less intense sunlight
   Cotton white colour clouds
   Which look good to eyes
   Breeze to feel good on skin
   And two times light shower
   Noon and after evening
   Flora makes surrounding good

4. *Look regular to bodily diseases*

5. *Look regular to bodily disorders*

6. *Treatment of body*
For diseases and disorders
A master way
When retain
Original body part
This a master mastery

7. *Finest fine joy*
Exist perfectly in own

8. *Health is*
A important thing
Joy or delight
Lives in healthy body

9. *Eyes and ears*
Are important senses
They are precious
Eyes and ears
Make the world
World form
From eyes and ears

10. *Good eye sight*
Makes world beautiful

At tenth is HUMAN RESEARCH

1. *For me*
   Exact things that hold
   My own finding

2. *Education*
   Where are
   Morals gesture
   Common things dead body dissolution

3. *For me*
   Knowledge of knows
   All must see
   Things through
   Their sense
   Do not believe
   On anything

4. *Your surrounding*
Is the book

5. *You are*
Writer of yourself

6. *You are world*

7. *Your sense is supreme*

8. *All things*
Start from you
And end with you
By your sense

9. *You take sense*
To infinite or limitless
And you are free

10. *Other things*
Are secondary
Your sense is supreme
And you are
Everything to yourself

11. *We are*
Capable of research

12. *We already arrive*
A long and easy life

At eleventh is HUMAN FEEL GOOD

1. *Feeling good*
   Is a feeling

2. *Age and its feel good*

3. *Three age feel good*

4. *Beginning age*
   Beginning age
   Is the
   First age stay
   Beginning age
   Feel good
   Is playing

5. *Marriage age*
Marriage age
Is the
Second age stay
Two live
In union
Marriage age
Happiness is
Twos union

6. *Parent age*
Parent age
Is the
Third age stay
Twos union
With their newborn
Parent age
Happiness is
Newborn or children

At twelfth is HUMAN DUTY

1. *In short say*
   Through parallel
   Practice sit silent
   And morals
   Practice to
   Hear parent
   And earn stand
   All the times
   For or With family
   Express above two
   Practices to society

2. *In detail say*
   To see education
   Education contain
   Human duty
   And morals
   Gesture common things
   Dead body dissolution

3. *Morals*

Blessing

I will always wish good to others

Consideration

I will always ponder on truth-

Form of content or form seeking no form

Considerable and truthful speak

I will always practice to speak in necessary only

I will always practice to speak softly

I will always speak truthful- sweet or good or right or to peace path

Mercy

I will always in practice to not disturb others

Help

I will always in practice through my capability

To do needful for a needy

Sacrifice

I will always be ready in parallel-

To sit silent and practice morals

To hear parent and earn stand all times for or with family

Express above two practices to society

Effortful

I will practice in slow manner continuous manner and by bodily active manner to complete any work

Goodwill

I will live a life by hard practice to not disturb others

Existing way

I will always in practice to maintain my good health

False neutralisation

Nil at this time

We see this later

Education

Share all these

So good appear everywhere
Sharing process of to know

4. **Gesture**
Two gestures
Gesture respecting others
My hand rise on heart to respect others

Gesture consideration
I walk calmly
And see and hear others calmly

5. *Good common things*
First common thing- Good food
Fruits milk staple food
Are good food

Second common thing- Good cloth
Two good clothes
Working cloth
Neck tight loose light cloth
Eyes shade cap
Gathering cloth
Neck tight good look giving cloth

Gathering cloth
Are society
Important discipline

Third common thing- Good house
Good house three things
Privacy
Surround cleanliness and beauty
And house beauty
House having yard
And connectivity by road
Road clean
And beautiful – decorous
House a precious part
Of human life
With deep attachment
Fourth common thing- Education
In short by two
Seeking Truth
Need fulfilment

Fifth common thing- Body health recovery
These are two
Medicine

And other means
Of recovery

Last common thing- Joy
All good sources of joy
Are integral parts of life

6. *Dead body dissolution*
Dead body with respect
Dissolve by special wood
Clean fire
Near river
Remains on cool
Leave to river water
Anyone can do process
Place arrangement by responsible

B

Be in silence always
Mind for deep observation

C

Be in silence
In non interpretation condition

Be in silence
In anger

Be in silence
In excitement

Focus on right result and dedicate
In fear

Focus on right result and dedicate
In attachment

Be in silence in grief
Practice for eternal
In ego

Try to forget
In lust

D

Interpret everything
Take right interpretation

E

Consider right interpretation
When fulfil need

And path values for fulfil need
Consideration
Considerable and truthful speak
Mercy
Help
Sacrifice
Effortful
Blessing
Goodwill
Existing way
False neutralisation
Education

F

On need fulfilment
Look as result of way